Parenting And Helping Kids With Dyslexia

A Parent's Guide to Nurturing a Dyslexic Child

Sharon M. Cheever

Copyright © 2023 Sharon M. Cheever

All rights reserved.

Table of Contents

Introduction

I believe it is reasonable to assume that parents of dyslexic children are more concerned about their kids than most. There is a strong explanation for this: dyslexic kids experience a lot of failure and difficulty throughout their early years in school.

When my kid was in the first grade, my anxiety peaked. During that academic year, assignments were less tolerant of his reading disability. His outstanding verbal vocabulary and sincere demeanor were no longer sufficient to divert attention from his mounting academic worries.

His confidence began to crumble, he became more insecure, and he lost interest in learning. Both his opinions of school and his capacity to connect with other students become more depressing. As his mother, I was at a loss as to where to direct my concern. Should anxiety about social, emotional, or intellectual matters take precedence? They all merged into a single, overwhelming anxiety because I was unable to choose one.

The unfortunate task of increasing our anxiety fell to our son's first-grade teacher. She had to give us some unpleasant news less than two months into first grade: not only was our kid struggling in reading, writing, and arithmetic, but he was also acting out. Playing up? I added behavioral concerns to my list after being devastated.

She was initially reluctant to give us the information, but we persisted. AppaOur had been caught robbing the school book fair of a book (I know) a book? It was an activity book with lots of graphics and little text, and he lied to another pupil about it. He hid in the boys' restroom out of humiliation until an adult arrived to bring him out. His instructor made an effort to comfort us by saying that young kids sometimes experiment with stealing and that it doesn't always imply anything. She cautioned us against overreacting and said that it was likely connected to his academic struggles in some way.

I became so depressed. How could he be failing on this level as well after all the effort we had put into encouraging his moral development? If our boy wasn't going to be an academic genius, at least we would make sure that he was chosen as a citizen of the month. I had already struck a deal with myself. I now had to include a moral concern in my list of worries.

My list of concerns became lengthy and lofty. I recall being concerned that my kid would never complete high school, let alone enroll in college. He was just seven.

In hindsight, my kid was merely a young boy going through a typical disruptive period brought on by his academic difficulties. Then, eleven years later, he received college admission. Stay with me on the journey to understanding dyslexia in children.

Chapter One

Understanding Dyslexia

Dyslexia is a reading and learning disability. People with dyslexia have difficulty reading quickly and correctly. They could also have trouble writing, spelling, and understanding what they read. These challenges, nevertheless, do not stem from a problem with intellect.

Dyslexia is a common condition that makes it difficult to interact with language. Some experts estimate that between 5 and 10 percent of people have it. Others estimate that up to 17% of people show signs of reading difficulty.

The effects of dyslexia do not go away with age. However, some educational strategies and procedures might aid in the student's growth as a reader and assist them in overcoming obstacles. Dyslexia tests may be given to people of any age, although they differ for adults and kids.

Reading fluently is often challenging for dyslexics. When they read slowly, they often make mistakes. That could have an impact on how well they can comprehend what they read. People often have no problem understanding the text when it is read to them. However, some individuals believe that dyslexia is a visual problem. For them, it resembles writing or flipping letters. Nevertheless, dyslexia is a language issue.

Although dyslexia has an impact on learning, it is important to realize that this is not a problem with intelligence. People with dyslexia are just as clever as their peers. Success stories involving dyslexics in the arts, business, and government are many.

Types of Dyslexia

Experts have classified some common types of dyslexia to increase the effectiveness of treatment. To best assist students, teachers may design approaches that are specific to their needs by understanding the many types of dyslexia.

Dyslexia with Dialects

This specific kind of dyslexia is often the first to spring to mind when the term is used. The difficulties of deciphering language sound and matching sounds to symbols are addressed. People with phonological dyslexia have trouble understanding or sounding out words. Phonological dyslexia is regarded as the most common kind of dyslexia. the following signs of phonological dyslexia:

- It might be difficult to learn letter combinations and letter sounds.
- difficulties with the pronunciation and spelling of foreign words.
- On the same page, there are several spellings of the same phrase.
- Refraining from reading when reading slowly.
- Having difficulty understanding familiar phrases in unexpected situations

Rapid Naming Dyslexia

People who struggle to rapidly recognize colors, numbers, and letters when they are presented with them may suffer from rapid naming dyslexia. This kind of dyslexia may have an impact on both reading speed and reading processing speed. Dyslexics with rapid naming can recognize colors, numbers, and letters, but it often takes them far longer to come up with the proper name. The following symptoms might result from rapid naming dyslexia:

- Having difficulty remembering words.
- Often changing words or leaving out words.
- Slow speech reaction makes it more challenging to complete reading or writing assignments.
- Utilizing body language instead of words to replace fake language with real language.

Dual Deficits Dyslexia

For someone with double-deficit dyslexia, two aspects of reading are challenging. Two of these aspects that are often addressed are the ability to recognize word sounds and naming speed. Although it is not common, this kind of dyslexia, which combines rapid naming and phonological processing, is sometimes regarded as the most severe. Signs of double deficit dyslexia include the following:

- Being unable to recall words quickly when requested to do so.
- Difficulties with phonological awareness.

Surface Dyslexia

Someone who finds it simple to sound out new words but finds it difficult to quickly recognize well-known ones may have surface dyslexia. In this case, experts argue that to process words quickly, the brain fails to recognize how a word looks. Because these words don't sound like their spellings, this kind of dyslexia makes it more difficult to sound out words that need to be taught. Surface dyslexia is sometimes known as visual dyslexia or dyskinetic dyslexia. It is common for a dyslexic individual to have both phonological and surface dyslexia. Some indications of surface dyslexia include:

- The completion of words is difficult to recognize.
- Reading slowly and avoiding reading activities.
- Having difficulties spelling.

Visual Dyslexia

Reading words that don't sound like their spellings may be difficult. The visual dyslexic has problems learning new words by sight. If a child has problems remembering what they have read on a page, they may have visual dyslexia. This kind of obstructs visual processing, depriving the brain of an accurate depiction of what the eyes see. Since learning to spell or form letters requires the brain to recall the proper letter sequence or shape, visual dyslexia will have an impact on acquiring these skills. These signs of visual dyslexia include:

- The text seems hazy or changes concentration sometimes.
- Tracking over several text lines is difficult.
- It's challenging to keep your position in the text.
- Headaches and/or eye strain caused by reading double text or writing that alternates between single and double

Categories of Dyslexia

Dyslexia in Development

Dyslexia that is genetically predisposed or present from birth is referred to as developmental dyslexia. Both primary and secondary dyslexia are categorized as developmental dyslexia. Boys are more likely than girls to have this kind of dyslexia, and it usually gets better as they become older.

Primary Dyslexia

It is referred to as primary dyslexia if the disorder that causes the dyslexia is genetically inherited. The likelihood that a kid will have dyslexia rises if both parents do. It's interesting to note that guys, particularly left-handed ones, are more likely to have primary dyslexia and that it may run in families.

Secondary Dyslexia

Early pregnancy-related issues with brain development may lead to secondary dyslexia. Since both primary and secondary dyslexia starts at birth, starts conditions are developmental.

Trauma Dyslexia

Dyslexia may sometimes emerge when sickness or severe brain injury damages the brain's language-processing regions. Because it is the only kind of dyslexia with a recognized etiology and is brought on by brain trauma, this kind of dyslexia is also known as trauma dyslexia.

Additional Learning Challenges Linked to Dyslexia

A person with dyslexia may also suffer some other learning challenges more often. In contrast to certain forms of dyslexia, they are neurological disorders, according to doctors. These learning challenges consist of:

Left-right Imbalance

Directional dyslexia is the term used to describe the inability to distinguish between left and right.

Dysgraphia

Word spacing, size, spelling, readability, and expressiveness are all impacted when people struggle with writing and other fine motor abilities.

Dyscalculia

A limitation on one's capacity for precise arithmetic computations, problem-solving, reasoning, understanding ideas relating to numbers, and mastering fundamental math abilities. Numeral or arithmetic dyslexia are other names for dyscalculia.

Disordered Processing of Audio

People who have auditory processing disorders have difficulty processing different speech sounds in their brains. Auditory dyslexia is another name for this disability.

Chapter Two

Symptoms and Causes

Dyslexia symptoms often start to show up in preschool. Here are the signs to watch out for, from early childhood through maturity, whether you're a parent, a teacher, or you suspect you could have dyslexia yourself.

The Years of Preschool

- Having trouble understanding popular nursery rhymes.
- Having trouble learning (and remembering) the alphabet's letter names.
- Being unable to distinguish the letters in one's name.
- Misspells well-known terms and uses a lot of "baby talk."

- Can not understand rhymes such as cat, bat, and rat.

- A history of reading or spelling issues in the family (dyslexia often runs in families);

Difficulties in Kindergarten and First Grade

- Does not comprehend how words may be broken apart.

- Complains about how difficult reading is and "disappears" when it's time to read; family history of reading difficulties;

- Unable to pronounce even basic terms like cat, map, and sleep.

- Doesn't connect letters to sounds, such as the letter b and the "b" sound.

- An illustrated page featuring a picture of a dog would say "puppy" instead of the written word "dog" due to reading mistakes that have no relation to the sounds of the letters on the page.

Strengths

- Curiosity
- Amazing imagination
- Logical thinking and grasp of the big picture
- Eager acceptance of new concepts
- A thorough comprehension of new ideas
- Unexpected maturity
- A vocabulary that is bigger than average for the age group
- Likes to solve problems
- Model-building talent
- Great understanding of tales read to him or spoken to him

Second Grade to High School

- Quite sluggish in learning to read. Reading is laborious and sluggish.

- Has difficulty reading unusual words and often makes assumptions because he cannot sound out the word.
- Doesn't seem to have a method for learning new words to read.
- Refrains from reading aloud
- Tries to find a precise phrase but ends up utilizing ambiguous words like "stuff" or "thing," without identifying the item
- Utilizes a lot of "um's" or pauses, hesitates, or other speech patterns while speaking
- Conflates similar-sounding terms, such as by stating "tornado" instead of "volcano" or "lotion" in place of "ocean."
- Mispronounced lengthy, strange, or difficult words
- Seems to need more time to answer inquiries
- Having trouble recalling names, phone numbers, dates, or random lists

- Struggles to complete exams on time struggles to learn a foreign language
- Errant spelling
- Illegible writing
- Self-esteem issues that may not be immediately apparent

Strengths

- Excellent mental, logical, creative, and abstract thinking abilities
- Meaningful learning is more effective than rote memory for learning.
- Understanding of the "big picture"
- A thorough comprehension of what is read to him
- The capacity to read and comprehend at a high level highly rehearsed (or overlearned) terms in a specialized field of interest; for instance, if they like cooking, they could be able to read food publications and cookbooks.

- Gain when a topic of interest gets more narrowly focused and specialized, as a small vocabulary is created to support reading in that subject.
- A remarkably complex vocabulary for listening
- Excels in disciplines that don't need reading, like math, computers, and the visual arts, or in courses that are more abstract than factual, like philosophy, biology, social studies, neuroscience, and creative writing.

Young Adults and Adults

- Reading
- Selling and reading history in childhood
- Even though reading abilities have improved over time, reading still involves a lot of work and is done slowly.

- Rarely reads for enjoyment
- Reading most things slowly, including books, manuals, and movie subtitles
- Refuses to read aloud
- Speaking
- Some of the earlier oral language issues are still present, such as a lack of fluency and glibness, a lot of "unprecise words, and overall uneasiness when speaking.
- Often mispronounces the names of people and places and stumbles over words.
- Inability to recall names of persons and locations; confusion between names that seem similar.
- Words are difficult to recall; there are many "it was on the tip of my tongue" moments.
- Rarely responds quickly in talks; difficulties when pressed for time

- Avoid using terms that might be mispronounced since spoken vocabulary is smaller than listening vocabulary.
- Despite having outstanding scores, he often claims to be stupid or worries that his friends will find him to be.
- Multiple-choice assessments penalize students
- Often forgoes social activities to focus on academics
- Extremely tired while reading; poor performance on routine clerical jobs

Strengths

- Keeps the skills that were noticed while you were school-age.
- Has a fast rate of learning.
- Increases significantly when given more time on multiple-choice tests.
- Exemplifies excellence while working in a highly specialized field like

fundamental science, law, public policy, economics, or medicine.

- Good writing abilities, as long as the emphasis is on the substance rather than the spelling.
- Very good at communicating thoughts and emotions.
- Outstanding kindness and sensitivity.
- Successful in areas that don't need rote memorization.
- High-level conceptualization skills and the capacity for innovative thought.
- The propensity to think creatively and holistically.
- Very adaptable and resilient.

Causes of Dyslexia

It's unclear what specifically causes dyslexia. However, various hints point to how and why the majority of instances occur.

Genetics

Highly inherited, dyslexia runs in families. A kid has a 30% to 50% probability of inheriting dyslexia if one parent has the condition. Dyslexia may also be more common in those who have genetic disorders like Down syndrome.

Variations in Brain Structure and Function

Having dyslexia makes you neurodivergent. That indicates that your brain is not wired or functioning as it should. According to research, people with dyslexia have altered brain chemistry, function, and structure.

disruptions in brain function and development. Events like infections, chemical exposures, and others may interfere with prenatal development and raise the risk that dyslexia will develop later in life.

Risk Factors

Several risk factors may affect a person's likelihood of developing dyslexia. They consist of:

Exposure to Toxins

Your chance of acquiring dyslexia may rise due to air and water pollution. This is particularly true for nicotine, some compounds used as flame retardants, and heavy metals (such as lead or manganese).

Absence of Reading Materials

Children who grow up in homes where reading isn't encouraged or where there isn't as much accessible reading material are more likely to acquire dyslexia.

Restrictions on the Learning Environment

Children who get less help for their learning in school or other comparable settings are more likely to acquire dyslexia.

Chapter Three

Myths About Dyslexia

This widespread learning discrepancy is still the subject of many myths. It may be challenging to determine what is true and the best way to help your kid as a result. Here are some dyslexia misconceptions debunked.

Myth: The primary indicator of dyslexia is the ability to read and write letters backward.
Fact: Some dyslexic children write their letters backward, while others do not. Letter reversal is thus not always an indication that your kid has dyslexia.

Young kids often reverse letters. It's not uncommon for kids to write p instead of q or mix up the letters b and d. But if your kid is still engaging in this behavior at the end of the first grade, it can be a hint that an assessment is required.

Myth: Dyslexia doesn't manifest until early childhood.

Fact: Dyslexia symptoms might appear as early as preschool. This is because dyslexia may impair language abilities, which are necessary for reading. A child who has trouble rhyming or who is a "late talker" may be at risk for dyslexia.

Myth: Vision issues cause dyslexia.

Fact: Dyslexia is not brought on by vision issues. Children who have dyslexia are not more likely than other children to develop eye and vision issues.

Indeed, certain people may have difficulty with their ability to interpret or perceive visual information. This indicates that the brain has problems digesting what the eyes see and identifying intricacies in pictures. These difficulties may make reading challenging. But they don't belong to dyslexia.

Myth: Dyslexic children only need to practice reading more.

The brains of children with dyslexia seem to work differently, according to research. It also demonstrates how reading may alter the brain over time. However, the effort has no bearing on it. Not how hard the pupils try, but the quality of education matters. Children with dyslexia may improve their reading skills over time with the right teaching and practice.

Numerous reading programs are available for readers who are having trouble. The so-called multimodal technique is often used. These three senses are used as learning tools in this form of training.

Myth: Once children learn to read, dyslexia disappears.

Fact: Intervention has a significant impact on helping dyslexic children learn to read. But just because they can read doesn't imply they've been "cured." Dyslexia is a lifelong learning disability that may have an impact on more than simply the ability to read fluently.

Dyslexia may make it challenging to read fluently in addition to making it challenging to decode. It could affect how effectively youngsters understand what they've read. Even when they have mastered reading, children with dyslexia may still have difficulties with spelling and writing.

Myth: A lack of reading time at home contributes to dyslexia.

All children should read at home and be introduced to reading, it is a fact. However, dyslexia is not caused by a lack of exposure. It is a neurological disorder. People who don't know your family can believe incorrectly that you aren't reading to your kid enough. You may have to explain that dyslexia is brought on by variations in how the brain works.

Myth: Only English speakers are susceptible to dyslexia.

It is a fact that dyslexia affects people everywhere and in all languages. But compared to their classmates, bilingual children often take longer to identify reading difficulties. This may be because parents and educators believe that the children are having difficulty. After all, they are learning a new language.

However, it's a good sign that children need to be checked if they struggle to read both in their native and second languages.

Chapter Four

Dyslexia Diagnosis

Dyslexia cannot be identified with a single test. There are several factors considered, including:

Your child's growth, academic difficulties, and medical history. A medical professional could ask you questions on these subjects. The provider will also want to know whether there are any family histories of issues, such as dyslexia or any other kind of learning impairment.

The provider may ask your child, caregivers, or teachers to respond to surveys. It could be necessary to test your child's language and reading abilities.

Tests for the brain (neurological), eyes, and hearing. These might help you determine if another issue is contributing to or exacerbating your child's reading challenges.

In a psychological evaluation, the doctor may quiz you and your child to find out more about their mental health. This might help you determine if your child's abilities are being restricted by social challenges, anxiety, or despair.

Assessments of intellectual capacity, such as reading. After passing a series of academic tests, your child's reading skills will be evaluated by a reading expert.

Chapter Five

The Impact Of Dyslexia On Learning

Your child's dyslexia will become more apparent in their schoolwork when they start to learn to read and write in elementary school. Dyslexia makes it more likely that your kid may take longer to complete written assignments or take notes since they may struggle to absorb fast language. School may be difficult for kids with dyslexia.

As previously mentioned, dyslexic children frequently struggle with other aspects of learning, such as knowing which is left from which, remembering the days of the week in order, and telling the time. They may also struggle with everyday tasks like tying their shoes or getting dressed. Due to these challenges, a dyslexic youngster may suffer from low self-esteem.

Dyslexic youngsters may struggle in school because they don't feel like the other students in their class. They may not like certain elements of school and struggle to reach their full potential in both their social and academic lives if they believe they are different from the other students in their class. Subjects like reading are quite challenging for children with dyslexia, and they often get irritated.

By letting them know that they are supported, working with your kid to assist their learning both at school and at home may help to build their sense of self-worth and confidence.

Observe your child's pace while you work with them. Instead of placing pressure on them, show them a lot of support and appreciation.

When reading to your child, keep in mind that kids with dyslexia have trouble seeing black text on a white backdrop; thus, utilizing colored films stretched over the page may help them read more easily.

Improve your child's handwriting together, making sure it is connected. Avoid teaching your kid to spell words by heart since they won't record them correctly. Instead, practice spelling patterns.

Make use of handwriting aids like large pens, paintbrushes, crayons, and various colored paper for your youngster to write on.

Read a lot of books together.
Use an egg timer to help your child learn about the passing of time.

Multisensory education is crucial. Try utilizing images, music, cartoons, inventing a game, or using art to create a notion if your youngster has trouble using words.

Having a positive connection with your dyslexic kid's school is essential because it will help ensure that your child has the greatest learning experience possible. This includes effective communication between you, the school's SENCO, and your child's class teacher. It's crucial to cultivate positive ties with the instructor and the school. Observe the home-schooling contract with the school. By assisting your dyslexic kid with their schoolwork, reading aloud often, practicing their times tables, and doing research on subjects, you may support their academic progress.

Good vocabulary skills are essential to preventing dyslexia from causing youngsters to lag in their education. Talk to your kid and encourage them to pursue their hobbies as this may aid in their reading development. At any age, share tales with your kid. Communicate often with the school about your kid's development and keep them updated, for instance, on how long it has taken your child to do their homework. Try to provide a quiet space for your kid to do their homework, and make sure it has been done and turned in. Specific structured interventions, such as that offered by DAS, will be most beneficial to your kid.

Consider the many instances of famous people who have tried to overcome dyslexia to help parents and kids realize that it is possible to succeed with the condition. Make an effort to preserve your child's self-esteem since it is crucial for success at all levels.

Chapter Six

How to Help Your Child

Dyslexic children provide special problems and possibilities for parents. You can create a dyslexia-friendly learning environment that supports your child's development and gives them the tools they need to realize their full potential as a committed parent. In this chapter, we'll look at useful techniques for helping your kid study efficiently and lay a solid academic foundation. You may help your kid learn by doing the following:

Creating a Learning Environment That is Dyslexia-Friendly:

Make sure your child has a peaceful, inviting location to work. reduce interruptions and provide them with a place where they may study without being disturbed.

Include visual signals in their learning environment because they matter. To make information more understandable and interesting, use charts, graphs, and color coding.

Accept Multisensory Methods: Recognize the advantages of multisensory teaching techniques for dyslexic students. Include multisensory activities in your curriculum, such as writing letters in sand or learning with tactile materials.

Selecting Effective Educational Interventions: Investigate the many educational interventions that are available for dyslexic children to learn more about your options for intervention. Take the time to do your research and speak with experts to identify the solution that best fits your kid's learning style since every child has different requirements.

Aiding Math, Writing, and Reading:

Use a variety of techniques to aid your child in learning to read. To improve their understanding, use phonics-based strategies, provide audiobooks, and encourage them to read aloud.

Fostering Writing Skills

Look at resources like speech-to-text software to assist your youngster in overcoming writing difficulties. Encourage them to come up with ideas vocally before writing them down.

Math Made Simple

Approach math with imagination and perseverance. Include practical examples and visual tools to help students comprehend arithmetic topics.

Increasing the Self-Esteem of Your Child:
Regardless of the result, acknowledge and compliment your child's efforts. Focusing on the advancements they make as they study can help you foster a growth mentality in your students.

Assist your youngster in identifying his or her talents and interests. Stress that their identity is more complex than simply having dyslexia and that they have special talents that show brightly.

Help your youngster learn to advocate for themselves. Encourage a feeling of autonomy in their learning by teaching children to express their wants and preferences.

By putting these techniques into practice, you're creating a safe and caring learning environment that will enable your child to grow despite the difficulties caused by dyslexia. Remember that their academic achievement and self-confidence are greatly influenced by your consistent support and commitment.

Chapter Seven

Working with the School

There has to be much more communication between parents and instructors. To get the greatest outcomes for your kid, regular, positive, and personal interaction with the classroom instructor is required. Teachers don't know your kid as well as you do, and most of them have only had very little special education training. Waiting for the teacher to contact you is unnecessary, especially if you have a kid who has special needs. Although they want to talk to the parents, it's acceptable if you call first. Help them; provide answers and tactics that you have successfully used at home.

Adhere to the chain of command. Talk to your child first. Wait to acquire additional details before getting in touch, whether it is concerning grades on the parent portal or anything they texted you about at school. While you should consider your child's explanation, remember that occasionally kids will simply provide their own opinions, which may not be entirely correct. Then, consult the instructor first if there is an issue that has to be resolved. You should only engage the principals or other administration as a last option. The majority of instructors aim for the highest levels of success, effectiveness, and positivity. It is unfair to involve the administration before the instructor has even been made aware of the problem.

Support the educators who work with your child. The individual you are interacting with is where they are at this very moment because they are passionately committed to assisting young learners. They are doing the best they can and primarily want the success of every youngster. These educators have a lot on their plate. As parents, it is your responsibility to provide your undivided attention to one kid. You are ensuring that the youngster is receiving the best care available. You keep track of your child's IEP, behavior, work, and other important details. Any error will be obvious to you, thus the best course of action is to be understanding. The most crucial rule is to never criticize your kid's teacher or their behavior in front of your child, even if it is inappropriate.

Be considerate. Be tolerant. Communicate and work together. Most educators are real about your child's success.

Chapter Eight

Conclusion

Let's think about the basic significance of optimism, hope, and your child's bright future as we come to the end of our trip through the pages of "Parenting and Helping a Dyslexic Child."

Keeping hope alive and having a positive outlook. The guiding light that helps us get through difficult times is hope. Keeping a positive mindset as a parent is essential for your child's development as well as for your person. Accept optimism as a motivating factor that will carry you on despite obstacles. Your unrelenting support and conviction in your child's potential may change their life.

Bringing to light the strengths of dyslexic children. We've looked at a variety of the strengths that kids with dyslexia have throughout this book. Their aptitude for creativity, problem-solving, and empathy is clearly evident. You may encourage an atmosphere where your kid can flourish and express themselves completely by recognizing and praising these qualities. Keep in mind that every obstacle they conquer serves as evidence of their tenacity.

There is no denying that kids with dyslexia have a bright future. The environment is altering, and more tools and resources are becoming accessible to aid in their ascent to success. As you now know, there are helpful therapies, encouraging educational strategies, and a greater understanding of the subtleties of dyslexia. Your dedication as a parent and advocate is crucial in helping your child realize their full potential.

You have a significant impact as a parent. You have given yourself the ability to parent your kid with wisdom, compassion, and unshakable love by taking in the information and techniques offered in this book. As you support their development, keep in mind that every action you take, every obstacle you conquer, and every happy time you spend with your kid helps to ensure their general well-being and future success.

Let's embrace hope as the cornerstone on which we construct a better future for our kids. Your commitment, coupled with your child's assets and aptitudes, will put them on a path to happiness and success. With the resources you've gathered, you're prepared to handle the challenges of raising a dyslexic child. Keep in mind that there are networks of support and understanding ready to travel this route with you.

We appreciate you joining us on this adventure. May optimism be your compass and the future a blank canvas for your child's ability to grow.

Dyslexia FAQ

Is dyslexia a result of trauma?

Yes, it has been suggested that trauma, both physical and emotional, may contribute to the development of dyslexia.

Traumatic dyslexia, also known as acquired dyslexia, may appear after a person has had a traumatic brain injury (TBI), which can be caused by accidents involving a vehicle, falls from ladders, sports injuries, etc. Traumatic dyslexia may develop as a consequence of a stroke or concussion. Trauma dyslexia may impact anyone, but it tends to affect adults more than kids.

On the other hand, psychological stress may also contribute to dyslexia. It is said that early exposure to stressful situations, such as emotional abuse, neglect, environmental catastrophe, bullying, seeing tragedy or death, etc., may result in dyslexia and other learning issues, even though there is little study on this sort of dyslexia.

What may someone with dyslexia see?
Every dyslexic person is different, and how they view things varies not simply based on the sort and degree of their dyslexia. One individual might be able to read numerals and characters backward or upside down, while another person would not be able to discern between letters like e, c, and o. Other times, the letters might look jumbled, out of sequence, or packed together. Although some dyslexics may struggle to sound out words and connect the letters, other dyslexics are able to do so without any problem.

When it comes to what a dyslexic person experiences or suffers from, there is no universal solution. The only way to be certain is to have a professional diagnosis, during which the doctor may carry out several tests, including word recognition, reading fluency and comprehension, decoding, spoken language abilities, and more.

Can dyslexia be cured?

Dyslexia cannot be outgrown and does not go away, but the difficulties that come with it may be greatly reduced with early intervention, the right teaching, and support. There are a variety of assistive technologies, such as text-to-speech, that may help accommodate people with dyslexia in addition to early intervention and assistance.

Does dyslexia just damage reading skills, or does it also influence speech?

Yes, dyslexia may impair one's capacity for speaking as well as reading. Delayed speech development in children is one of the early indicators of dyslexia. Children with dyslexia may have a variety of speech problems in addition to this delay, including stuttering or speech insufficiency, decreased phonological awareness, diminished phonological recall, jumbling up similar-sounding words, and poor phonological awareness.

A child's ability to speak may be less negatively impacted by dyslexia by participating in speech therapy under the supervision of a certified speech-language pathologist. SLPs may support early language development and assist in evaluating a child's reading and writing skills.

Can dyslexia emerge later in life?
Most dyslexics are born with the condition, however, dyslexia may also appear later in life. As mentioned above, traumatic brain damage, such as a stroke or concussion, is the most common cause of this late-onset condition. On

the other hand, it's more likely that you've had dyslexia throughout your life and it wasn't discovered until much later if you were only diagnosed as an adult and haven't had a catastrophic brain injury.

What should you do if you think you may have dyslexia?

Start by discussing your worries with your primary care physician. Developmental delays, behavioral concerns, or mental health problems may all be causes for concern. Ask your child's teacher about their academic performance, social interactions, and any difficulties the staff may have noticed. To confirm a dyslexia diagnosis, ask for further testing, either via your family doctor or your child's school.

Your kid will have a personalized learning plan created by the school after their dyslexia has been confirmed and the type has been determined. You might look for alternate therapies outside the confines of the classroom.

www.ingramcontent.com/pod-product-compliance
Lightning Source LLC
Chambersburg PA
CBHW070959250726
48663CB00002B/290